Weather Watch

Fog

by Jenny Fretland VanVoorst

Bullfrog Books

Ideas for Parents and Teachers

Bullfrog Books let children practice reading informational text at the earliest reading levels. Repetition, familiar words, and photo labels support early readers.

Before Reading

- Discuss the cover photo. What does it tell them?

- Look at the picture glossary together. Read and discuss the words.

Read the Book

- "Walk" through the book and look at the photos. Let the child ask questions. Point out the photo labels.

- Read the book to the child, or have him or her read independently.

After Reading

- Prompt the child to think more. Ask: Have you ever been in a really thick fog? How far could you see in front of you?

Bullfrog Books are published by Jump!
5357 Penn Avenue South
Minneapolis, MN 55419
www.jumplibrary.com

Library of Congress Cataloging-in-Publication Data

Names: Fretland VanVoorst, Jenny, 1972– author.
Title: Fog / by Jenny Fretland VanVoorst.
Description: Minneapolis, MN: Jump!, Inc. [2016]
Series: Weather watch | Audience: Ages 5–8.
Includes index. | Description based on print version record and CIP data provided by publisher; resource not viewed.
Identifiers: LCCN 2016016183 (print)
LCCN 2016015825 (ebook)
ISBN 9781624964350 (ebook)
ISBN 9781620313886 (hardcover: alk. paper)
Subjects: LCSH: Fog—Juvenile literature.
Classification: LCC QC929.F7 (print)
LCC QC929.F7 F74 2016 (ebook)
DDC 551.57/5—dc23
LC record available at
https://lccn.loc.gov/2016016183

Editor: Kirsten Chang
Series Designer: Ellen Huber
Book Designer: Molly Ballanger
Photo Researcher: Olympia Shannon

Photo Credits: All photos by Shutterstock except: Age Fotostock, 4; Deposit Photos, 12–13, 23tr; Dreamstime, 8–9, 18, 22tl, 23br; Getty, 6–7; iStock, 10, 11, 14–15, 23tl; Thinkstock, 3, 19, 20–21.

Printed in the United States of America at Corporate Graphics in North Mankato, Minnesota.

Table of Contents

A Foggy Day 4

Foggy Places 22

Picture Glossary 23

Index 24

To Learn More 24

A Foggy Day

What a foggy day!
How far can you see?

Not very far.
Why?

You are looking
through a cloud!

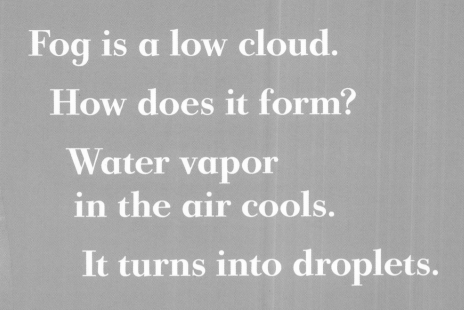

Fog is a low cloud.
How does it form?
Water vapor
in the air cools.
It turns into droplets.

droplets

When this happens
high in the air,
it makes a cloud.

When it happens near the ground, it makes fog.

11

Some places are foggier than others.

Where? Valleys.

Near water.

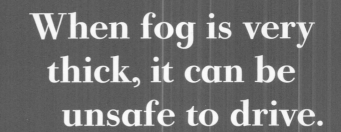

When fog is very thick, it can be unsafe to drive.

Airplanes can't take off.

School may be delayed.

When sun warms
the air, the fog lifts.

Hello, sun!

Foggy Places

valleys

lakes

seashores

cities

Picture Glossary

cloud
A visible mass of particles of water or ice, usually high in the air.

valley
A low area between ranges of hills or mountains.

droplets
Very small drops.

vapor
Fine particles of a liquid, such as water, that are suspended in the air.

Index

air 9, 10, 21

airplanes 18

cloud 6, 9, 10

droplets 9

ground 11

school 19

seeing 4

sun 21

thick 17

valleys 13

vapor 9

water 9, 14

To Learn More

Learning more is as easy as 1, 2, 3.

1) Go to www.factsurfer.com

2) Enter "fog" into the search box.

3) Click the "Surf" button to see a list of websites.

With factsurfer.com, finding more information is just a click away.